BIGGEST NAMES IN MUSIC

# SHAWN MENDES

by Emma Huddleston

FOCUS
READERS.
NAVIGATOR

# WWW.FOCUSREADERS.COM

Focus Readers is distributed by North Star Editions:
sales@northstareditions.com | 888-417-0195

Produced for Focus Readers by Red Line Editorial.

Photographs ©: Evan Agostini/Invision/AP Images, cover, 1, 19; Chris Pizzello/Invision/AP Images, 4–5, 20–21; Amy Harris/Invision/AP Images, 7; Matt Sayles/Invision/AP Images, 8, 25; Arthur Mola/Invision/AP Images, 10–11, 27; Mark Blinch/The Canadian Press/AP Images, 12; Drew Gurian/Invision/AP Images, 14–15; Kevin Mazur/The Recording Academy/Getty Images Entertainment/Getty Images, 17; Shutterstock Images, 23, 29

**Library of Congress Cataloging-in-Publication Data**
Names: Huddleston, Emma, author.
Title: Shawn Mendes / by Emma Huddleston.
Description: Lake Elmo, MN : Focus Readers, 2021. | Series: Biggest names in music | Includes index. | Audience: Grades 4-6
Identifiers: LCCN 2020008542 (print) | LCCN 2020008543 (ebook) | ISBN 9781644936375 (hardcover) | ISBN 9781644936467 (paperback) | ISBN 9781644936641 (pdf) | ISBN 9781644936559 (ebook)
Subjects: LCSH: Mendes, Shawn, 1998---Juvenile literature. | Singers--Canada--Biography--Juvenile literature.
Classification: LCC ML3930.M444 H83 2021  (print) | LCC ML3930.M444 (ebook) | DDC 782.42164092 [B]--dc23
LC record available at https://lccn.loc.gov/2020008542
LC ebook record available at https://lccn.loc.gov/2020008543)

Printed in the United States of America
Mankato, MN
082020

## ABOUT THE AUTHOR

Emma Huddleston lives in the Twin Cities with her husband. She enjoys writing children's books and staying active. She thinks music is an important part of life and spends some afternoons learning how to play the piano.

# TABLE OF CONTENTS

# CHAPTER 1

# AWARD-WINNING DUET

Thousands of people filled the theater at the 2019 American Music Awards (AMAs). The huge crowd clapped and cheered. Their eyes were fixed on the long stage. Shawn Mendes stood at one end, holding his guitar. Camila Cabello posed at the other end. The lights were low.

Camila Cabello and Shawn Mendes sing their hit song "Señorita" at the AMAs.

5

The duo was performing their song "Señorita." Cabello sang first. Her red dress swayed as she walked toward Mendes. The band played a slow rhythm. People in the crowd waved their hands back and forth.

Then, the beat picked up. Mendes strummed his guitar. He turned toward

## CAMILA CABELLO

Cabello and Mendes started dating in 2019. But they had met several years earlier. They recorded the hit song "I Know What You Did Last Summer" back in 2016. Like Mendes, Cabello has a successful career on her own. "Havana" is one of her biggest hits. This song came out in 2017. It topped charts in the United States and around the world.

Cabello and Mendes perform together at the Jingle Ball in December 2015.

the microphone and starting singing. His smooth voice floated over the crowd. Red and orange lights flashed behind him.

"Señorita" won Best Collaboration at the MTV Video Music Awards in 2019.

Cabello danced as Mendes sang. Then she joined him for the chorus. The two singers gazed at each other as they sang.

They danced and swayed together. Then they moved in close and faced each other. Cabello held her microphone in between their mouths so they could sing the last few words together.

The music faded, and the crowd roared. Mendes and Cabello smiled at each other, then out to the crowd. Everyone loved their romantic performance.

Mendes is one of the biggest names in music. "Señorita" was voted the No. 1 song in the United Kingdom. And it won **Collaboration** of the Year at the AMAs. But the duet was not Mendes's only hit. At age 20, he already had a successful **solo** career.

# CHAPTER 2

# DISCOVERING MUSIC

**S**hawn Peter Raul Mendes was born on August 8, 1998, in Toronto, Ontario. He and his younger sister Aaliyah grew up in the nearby city of Pickering.

As a kid, Shawn enjoyed sports and playing outside. He first got involved in music at Pine Ridge Secondary School.

Shawn plays a concert in Toronto, Ontario, in October 2015.

Shawn played both ice hockey and soccer in high school.

Shawn took a musical theater class. He practiced singing, dancing, and acting. The class became his favorite. It inspired him to learn guitar. Shawn taught himself how to play by watching YouTube videos.

Less than a year later, Shawn started posting his own videos to YouTube.

He sang or played guitar. He often did covers of popular songs. A cover is when someone performs a song that was originally by someone else.

At first, only a few people watched Shawn's videos. But that was all about to change.

## WORKING HARD ON THE ICE

Shawn started playing hockey when he was 13 years old. At first, he wasn't very good. Sometimes his teammates didn't pass the puck to him because they worried he might mess up. But instead of quitting, Shawn worked hard to improve. He practiced with his dad after school. In time, he became one of the best players on the team.

# SINGING COVERS

In August 2013, Shawn posted a cover of "As Long as You Love Me" by Justin Bieber. When Shawn woke up the next day, he couldn't believe what had happened. The video already had more than 10,000 likes. Its success helped Shawn gain thousands of followers on social media.

Shawn posted his cover to Vine. This app let people share short six-second videos.

Three months later, Andrew Gertler found one of Shawn's videos online. Gertler worked in the music industry. He thought Shawn had talent. So, he helped Shawn get a meeting with Island Records. That company helps singers make and sell music. If the meeting went well, it could help Shawn start his career.

At the meeting, Shawn performed a few songs for **producers**. He played some covers and some songs he wrote himself. The producers were impressed with Shawn's voice and talent. They offered him a **record deal**. Shawn signed it in May 2014. He was just 15 years old. The deal put pressure on him to succeed.

Andrew Gertler (right) became Shawn's manager. He joined Shawn and Shawn's dad at the Grammys in 2019.

The young singer was both nervous and excited.

A month later, Shawn released his first **single**, "Life of the Party." In a week, it reached No. 24 on *Billboard*'s Hot 100.

This list tells which songs are bought and played the most in the United States. Shawn was the youngest person ever to reach one of the top 25 spots with a **debut** song. From there, his fame continued to grow. For example, *Time* magazine named him one of the 25 Most Influential Teens of 2014.

Next, Shawn released a full-length album. *Handwritten* came out in April 2015. The album included his early singles and some new songs. It reached No. 1 on *Billboard*'s list after only one week. In May 2015, Shawn's third single, "Stitches," rocked the charts. It reached No. 4 in its first week. That made it

Shawn opened for Taylor Swift during her worldwide tour in 2015.

Shawn's first Top 10 single. One fan of his music was Taylor Swift. She invited Shawn to be an opening performer on her tour that year. Shawn gained more fans while traveling and performing with Swift.

# CHAPTER 4

# WORLD TOURS AND TOP AWARDS

**M**endes's music continued to attract more fans. By 2016, he'd won the People's Choice Award for Favorite Breakout Artist. One song that led to his popularity was "Treat You Better." This song spoke out against **abusive** relationships. It sent an important message about respecting other people.

Mendes accepts the People's Choice Award for Favorite Breakout Artist in 2016.

The song was part of his second album, *Illuminate*. This album came out in September 2016.

The next year, Mendes went on his first world tour. He started in April in Glasgow, Scotland. Eight months later, the tour ended in Tokyo, Japan. At each show,

## FRIENDLY TO FANS

Mendes is known for being honest and polite. He rarely turns down a chance to meet fans and take selfies with them. And he is very active on social media. Mendes posts photos and videos of his daily life. He also responds to messages from fans. This open, friendly approach is very popular with his fans. By 2020, he had more than 55 million followers on Instagram.

Mendes performs at the VillaMix Festival in Brazil in 2018.

Mendes built deeper connections with fans. Large crowds clapped and cheered when he was onstage. Offstage, Mendes met fans in person. He also kept fans up to date by posting on social media.

His third album, *Shawn Mendes*, came out in May 2018. For this album, Mendes let some of his life experiences influence his songwriting. For example, "In My Blood" tells about his struggle with anxiety. Fans loved how the **lyrics** gave an inside look at Mendes's life. To many listeners, the new songs felt more personal and honest. And people who faced similar struggles could relate to Mendes.

Critics noticed the new depth of his music, too. In 2018, Mendes earned his first two Grammy **nominations**. The Grammys are a major music award show. Being nominated is a great honor.

Mendes sings "In My Blood" with Miley Cyrus at the 61st Grammy Awards.

Mendes's song "In My Blood" was nominated for Song of the Year. And *Shawn Mendes* was nominated for Best Pop Vocal Album. Although Mendes didn't win either award, it was still a big moment in his career.

Mendes had several other important successes. He won the People's Choice Award for Male Artist in both 2018 and 2019. Fans also voted for him at the Teen Choice Awards. Mendes won three of those awards in 2019. And his song "Señorita" with Camila Cabello received a Grammy nomination.

Mendes wants to use his fame to make positive change in the world. In August 2019, he started the Shawn Mendes Foundation. The charity gives money to causes that are important to Mendes and his fans. For example, it has supported mental health research and children's hospitals. It also gave money to help

Mendes poses with fans during WE Day. This event inspires young people to help their communities.

build schools in Ghana and to protect the environment.

In 2020, Mendes continued touring around the world and working on his next album. Fans couldn't wait to see what the young star would do next.

# SHAWN MENDES

- Birth date: August 8, 1998
- Birthplace: Toronto, Ontario, Canada
- Family members: Karen (mother), Manuel (father), Aaliyah (sister)
- High school: Pine Ridge Secondary School
- Major accomplishments:
  - August 2013: Mendes's cover video of "As Long as You Love Me" gets more than 10,000 likes overnight.
  - June 2014: Mendes releases his first single, "Life of the Party."
  - April 2015: Mendes releases his first full-length album, *Handwritten*.
  - January 2016: Mendes wins the People's Choice Award for Favorite Breakout Artist.
  - November 2019: "Señorita" earns Mendes and Camila Cabello a Grammy nomination.

Mendes performs at the iHeartRadio Music Festival in Las Vegas, Nevada.

- Quote: "[My fans'] energy and dedication to improving the world is so incredible, and I am hoping we can use [the Shawn Mendes Foundation] as a way to lift each other up, learn together, and inspire more people to get involved in giving back."

Raisa Bruner. "Shawn Mendes Doubles Down on Charity with the Shawn Mendes Foundation." *Time*. Time USA, 28 Aug. 2019. Web. 24 Feb. 2020.

# FOCUS ON
# SHAWN MENDES

*Write your answers on a separate piece of paper.*

1. Write a paragraph explaining the main ideas of Chapter 3.

2. If you were famous, would you share lots of posts about your daily life with fans? Why or why not?

3. What was the first single Mendes released?

   **A.** "Life of the Party"
   **B.** "Stitches"
   **C.** "Señorita"

4. How can posting on social media help an artist's music career?

   **A.** People will view the posts instead of attending the artist's concerts.
   **B.** People can't steal the artist's ideas for songs.
   **C.** People will view the posts and learn about the artist's music.

*Answer key on page 32.*

# GLOSSARY

**abusive**
Violent or cruel.

**collaboration**
A project where two or more people work together.

**debut**
The first of something.

**lyrics**
The words of a song.

**nominations**
When people, songs, or albums are chosen as finalists for an award or honor.

**producers**
People who work with musicians to record songs.

**record deal**
An agreement where an artist makes an album that a company sells and promotes.

**single**
A song that is released on its own.

**solo**
Performing alone, not as part of a group.

# TO LEARN MORE

## BOOKS

Caravantes, Peggy. *Shawn Mendes: Pop Star*. Mankato, MN: The Child's World, 2017.

Huddleston, Emma. *Taylor Swift*. Lake Elmo, MN: Focus Readers, 2021.

Rector, Rebecca Kraft. *Shawn Mendes: Singer-Songwriter*. New York: Enslow Publishing, 2019.

## NOTE TO EDUCATORS

Visit **www.focusreaders.com** to find lesson plans, activities, links, and other resources related to this title.

# INDEX

**Answer Key: 1.** Answers will vary; **2.** Answers will vary; **3.** A; **4.** C